Always
Italicise

Always Italicise

how to write while colonised
Alice Te Punga Somerville

UNIVERSITY OF HAWAI'I PRESS
Honolulu

First published in 2022 by
Auckland University Press
University of Auckland
Private Bag 92019
Auckland 1142
New Zealand

www.aucklanduniversitypress.co.nz

Published in 2024 in North America by
University of Hawaiʻi Press
2840 Kolowalu Street
Honolulu, HI 96822

www.uhpress.hawaii.edu

ARTS COUNCIL OF NEW ZEALAND TOI AOTEAROA

Published with the assistance of Creative New Zealand

Library of Congress Cataloging-in-Publication Data
Names: Te Punga Somerville, Alice, author.
Title: Always italicise : how to write while colonised / Alice Te Punga
  Somerville.
Description: Honolulu : University of Hawaiʻi Press, [2023] | First
  published in 2022 by Auckland University Press. | Poems in English with
  some Māori words.
Identifiers: LCCN 2023021452 | ISBN 9780824897369 (paperback)
Subjects: LCSH: Māori (New Zealand people)—Ethnic identity—Poetry. |
  Postcolonialism—New Zealand—Poetry. | LCGFT: Poetry.
Classification: LCC PR9639.4.T4 A78 2023 | DDC 821/.92—dc23/eng/20230601
LC record available at https://lccn.loc.gov/2023021452

Cover design by Neil Pardington
Internal design by Katie Kerr

This book was printed on FSC® certified paper. University of Hawaiʻi Press
books are printed on acid-free paper and meet the guidelines for permanence
and durability of the Council on Library Resources.

Printed in Singapore by Markono Print Media Pte Ltd

For Titilia Ngaere *Vakarau —*
may you **bold** *and* <u>underline</u> *always.*

Contents

Reo

on the back of a fish
I walk with my tongue cut out

— Apirana *Taylor,* <u>He Tangi Aroha</u>

Tōku reo, tōku ohooho.

— Whakataukī

By choosing to write in English,
Māori *writers lessen the chances*
of survival for the Māori *language.*

— Hirini *Melbourne,* 'Whare whakairo:
  Maori *"literary" traditions'*

Kupu rere kē

My friend was advised to italicise all the foreign words in her poems.
This advice came from a well-meaning woman
with NZ poetry on her business card
and an English accent in her mouth.

I have been thinking about this advice.

The convention of italicising words from other languages
clarifies that some words are imported:
it ensures readers can tell the difference between a foreign language
and the language of home.

I have been thinking about this advice.

Marking the foreign words is also a kindness:
every potential reader is reassured
that although you're expected to understand the rest of the text,
it's fine to consult a dictionary or native speaker for help with the italics.

I have been thinking about this advice.

Because I am a contrary person, at first I was outraged —
but after a while I could see she had a point:
when the foreign words are camouflaged in plain type
you can forget how they came to be there, out of place, in the first place.

I have been thinking about this advice
and I have decided to follow it.

Now all of my readers will be able to remember
which words truly belong in Aotearoa *and which do not.*

Layers

(for Vula)

Our language is in triplicate:
Like those old accounting notebooks
With different coloured pages
Nestled one on top of the other
Over and over again;
A concertina, geological time on a rockface, a lei.

The writing looks different each time:
Dark pen on top layer
Clear copy next
And finally, underneath, a scratched barely legible pattern
Readable only if you know what you're looking for,
More faith and hope than ink.

Frustrated with the chore of reading
I argue first and second layers are adequate:
Two languages are more than enough to teach our child;
You gently urge me to persevere
Not directly, but by your own focused study of letters barely there,
Knowing – so I realise – that in faint outlines and mere impressions
You'll find the heart of me.

Rākau

We know that carvers coax something or someone
Who's already there in the wood
They remove small pieces of timber, one by one, until it's ready.

We both know a language is waiting inside my tongue.

Please put down the adze, the skillsaw, the file
Speak gently to me so I can recognise what's there.

No, don't chip away at pink flesh and taste buds:
Oozing and swollen, I will choke on my blood before you're done.

The wood you're trying to carve is still a tree.

Kei te mōhiotia ko te kaiwhakairo tērā ka kukume mai
i te mauri o roto rawa i te rākau.
Ka tangohia kōtirihia ngā kongakonga rākau,
kia reri ai.

Kei te mōhio tāua, he reo kei tōku arero.

Waiho ki raro te toki, te kani, te whaiuru:
kōrerotia whakamāriretia kia kite ai au he aha rā kei reira.

Kāo, kaua e tope i te kiko māwhero, i ngā paerongo tāwera:
e totō ana pūpuhi nei, kei rāoa au e aku toto
i mua iho i tō otinga noa.

Ko te rākau e ngana ana koe ki te whakairo he rākau tonu.

(*Translation:* Te Ataahia Hurihanganui)

red-carded

your nametag is red because you don't speak your own language
it is not enough for you to hold this secret tightly: everyone must know

red like the adulterer's A
marked, branded, tagged for identification upon recapture

hangs around your neck like a millstone;
       you are thrown into the harbour with rocks tied around your body:
       your grandfather's humiliation, your mother's hurt,
       the inheritance your children won't be getting

hangs around your neck like a noose;
       the weight of them all:
       all your family, so many friends, hanging off the lanyard too
       when the stool is kicked out the way at least it will be quick

your nametag is red

why wear your heart on your sleeve
when you can wear your shame on your chest?

ielts

i am writing a poem
on the notes app on my phone
while i wait to start a test
so i can migrate to a country
that demands proficiency in english
or french

what humour is this
the girl who only speaks english
with a phd in english
having to prove
she knows english

what empire is this
a māori *woman*
moving to musqueam territory
handing her new zealand passport
to be checked by women
with southern africa and southeast asia
in their mouths

what violence is this
sitting in air conditioning
on whenua māori
matekai ki taku reo tūturu
taku reo rangatira

what whakamā

burdens for this generation

(for Matiu *and* Tamati*)*

i've heard about the heaviness:

the weight of European Imperialism
on the shoulders of the Māori-speaking child
standing in the entrance to the schoolroom:

leaning on the doorjamb   *one language for one side and one for the other*
lovingly pushed by well-meaning families   *into a room that turned out to be an abyss*

another burden:

> *the silence of a kuia whose daughter*
>   *attempts a karanga for them all*
> *the nervousness of a brave cousin*
>   *holding lines on a slip of paper*
> *the whispers and prods and looking around*
>   *the shame of having to explain*

piled like the shoes and jackets at the door
half-warming half-smothering a three-year-old child

Anchor

Before you were born, we decided you would be our weapon
Our strategy
Our bullet-proof vest.

You would speak the language that we could not.

And, by so doing, would right the wrongs
or turn back time
or some other cliché about gently nudging recent ancestors
who loved us by pretending they couldn't speak it either.

It was unfair: a newborn baby taking a first breath
surrounded by adults wanting to trick you into believing in a world
which for us remained a fantasy.

Wanting your every utterance to be different from our own:
picking up shame from where it has pooled around our feet;
scooping it into buckets, or bailers, or cups;
holding it out for you to make it all disappear.

You were our baby in the manger:
the one whose tongue would save us all.

———

Over time we have come to know that words on the page are unkind to you.

You know so much of two spoken languages
but Māori boys at school are not judged for poetry.

These adults in your life still as hopeless as ever
waving to you in your world across a thin crack which some days feels like a ditch.

We read earnest articles about the importance of reading.
We panic about future gaps at high school and fear you could slip between them.

We sit in our houses of books and try to find the line
between reading as medicine and reading as punishment.

————

And then you skype with me late one afternoon to practise your speech
which begins with your pepeha *as if that is the most ordinary way to start*
when you're eleven years old.

How were we to know — to even guess — that this language would be your weapon
Your strategy
Your bullet-proof vest.

flight

they're good people
i had a few of them work for me

      things overheard
      at an airport bar

people going to kerrykerry
wonn-grey wockatarny

      things announced
      at the gate

the clipping of wings
the breaking of necks

Invisible Ink

*Indeed, the natural, everyday presence
of the 'way things are' explains the strength
and resilience of racism. Racism envelops us,
intoxicating our thoughts, permeating our
brains and skins, determining the shape of
our growth and the longevity of our lives.*

— Haunani-Kay Trask, *'The Color of Violence'*

It's racist as fuck.

— Taika Waititi, *'Unknown Mortal Orchestra* & Taika Waititi
   on New Zealand culture'

*I've long had to theorise the material and
epistemological bruises upon my body . . .
I thought if I understood the violence,
I could parry the blow.*

— Chelsea Watego (Bond), *'Talkin' down to the Black Woman'*

mad ave

i.

dave dobbyn wrote a song about madeleine avenue.
dlt helped him out with it
and it's a good song

to those of us who grew up in the area,
the street they sing about wasn't 'madeleine avenue' —
it couldn't carry off that kind of name.

it was mad ave.

ii.

parallel to mad ave was esperance,
the road we walked along after school.
we'd start off a big group
talking and laughing and yelling 'see ya'
as kids peeled off to their houses.

because my street came off the other end of esperance,
i'd walk all the way to the end.

iii.

walking home was always a bit scary because of the dogs.
sometimes i'd imagine a dog waiting till i was all alone
choosing that as the time to attack.

my friend stephanie's big sister saw a dog run over on esperance once.
the car ran straight over its stomach,
then the dog jumped up and kept running down the street.
we would tell and retell that story,
shaking our heads, laughing at that kind of dog
— 'those dogs on esperance man' —

impressed by the sheer resilience of the unsquashable dog
horrified it might still be out there

the dog that i was most scared of wasn't unknown:
the dog i was most scared of was max,
the giant black dog that hid behind mrs mafileo's flowers,
and when camille and i used to leave school at lunchtime
to visit our friend tasha and baby jessie,
we'd walk up the steps
holding on to each other
stomachs in our throats,
wondering if max's head was going to pop up behind the chrysanthemums.

iv.

with tasha we'd drink diet coke and watch oprah or days of our lives.
i didn't always go back to school afterwards,
when i did i'd sometimes have jessie's milky sick
on the shoulder of my regulation blouse
if it was really bad i'd cover it
with tasha's old school uniform jumper.

i remember the time tasha brought jessie to school
and that principal of ours who'd been so mean and inflexible
during the pregnancy
asked tasha if he could hold baby.
as soon as she was in his arms,
jessie turned her little head
and sicked on his pristine shirt sleeve.

v.

the flats on mad ave and esperance
were emptied out

boarded up
and then
gone.

mum says the saddest thing
was seeing the taro patches
who didn't know to stop growing:
weedy offcuts of gardens
resistance of leaves and stems.

vi.

the last time i was in new zealand i drove through mad ave.
it's not called mad ave anymore —
it's mount taylor drive, thank you very much,
after the english name for taurere,
the mountain that's really much closer to a molehill
and sits doggedly at the end of the street.

mount taylor drive is a bit different to mad ave.

each house takes up the space of three or four mad ave families
there aren't any cars on blocks in the front yard,
there are no taro patches in the back
old ladies chatting as they walk up the road
kids walking home from school,
no dogs or chrysanthemums,
and though i'm sure the new places don't have the rot
or worn-out-ness
that the old places had,
to me they look like a gust of wind
might make the walls topple over
the roof fall in
the windowpanes crash to the ground.

'mount taylor drive' isn't a change of name for the same street
as much as it's a new name for a new thing.

vii.

when i was 14
i was in a school production about taurere
and the stories told about the people who'd known the landscape
before mad ave, before mount taylor drive.

i'm still not sure who has the right to mourn
who has the right to say
that their place was taken away.

This is what it feels like

This is what it feels like to be the only Māori person
in your workplace:

everyone else heads out for an impromptu lunch
on one of the first real days of summer

they make plans and rush
up and down corridors
            (up down up down)
up and down stairs
            (up down up down)
they pile into the lift
            (down)

meanwhile, my door has been open the whole time.

I've been in here, writing the acknowledgements
for an essay I'm going to send to a journal
I've been naming the communities of Indigenous scholars
feeling warm about the places I've been,
the people who have been generous and listened to my ideas.

My door has been open the whole time
while they've rushed around
and when the last person calls out 'okay are we all here?'
I know they think they're all there:
everyone is there.

That's what it feels like.

This is what it sounds like:

(silence).

serenity prayers   *(for Titilia)*

i can only hope that this baby
won't be followed around the inside of shops to check for stealing
won't be pulled over for driving too flash a car
won't be ridiculed for wearing the wrong skin

fleet

you sit outside a prison, watching miracles:

visitations
> *of a different kind.*

the inexplicable faith of families

a carparkful of departures:
> *the planning of journeys*
>> *to this complicated system of locks and gates*

everything is angles,
> *except for loops of wire and*
>> *a small carving*

a polynesian destination for these centuries:
> *arrivals to a bigger*
>> *colder place*

1 September 2008

An astronomy of politics:
the alignment of stars

What good could come
of this triple constellation?

high court hearings for people
extracted
from early morning beds almost a year ago:
the wisdom teeth of the state
or the DNA sequence that tells us who we are?

the launch of a book of words:
a dictionary more full
of my grandfather's language
than any has been before.
i'm terrified
i won't ever use it:
too powerful medicine
for my quiet limping tongue

the last chance to buy a ticket
for the tribunal raffle:
gifts of precious naked stories
in exchange for the chance to win a hamper
brimming with the contents
of our own cupboards:
no way to get another ticket
for what we haven't yet noticed is missing

birthday milestones
are such selfish things

turning thirty-three
such an irrelevant act

a new generation of historians on flight NZ449   (for Aroha)

it's complimentary happy hour:
little plates of cheese, and wine or beer in plastic cups

smiling people who can serve us in english, french or japanese
even though there's a koru on the tail of this plane.

a trivia game, asinine questions for suburbandog millionaires
small hanging screens cycling through a series of claims about the world:

which is further west: chad, oman or mali?
                on a plane that speaks three languages
                        from north of the equator;
                on a world that isn't flat anymore,
                        where everywhere is further west than somewhere.

a question about tommy solomon the last full-blooded moriori
                they expect no one from rēkohu
                        to decide between sav and merlot on this trip;
                a quiet dismantling,
                        pruning unfruitful wood from national vines.

i have to fill this plane with other words.

writing on a sickbag, i wonder if these pencil marks
would dissolve or be more stark
if i filled the bag with what it is designed to hold:
liquefied wests, regurgitated lasts.

we are, after all, in a plane with a koru on its tail.

Waitangi *Day 2019*

You walked out to the car
as soon as you heard me pull in the driveway.

      Do you talk to your landlord often?

I had left for Auckland at 6am with a grieving husband
so he could fly home to bury his grandmother.

I was exhausted, even with two coffees on board,
and buckled-in baby had just woken again.

      Who?
      Your landlord . . .

Then something about the way our tree should be trimmed
where it hangs over your driveway.

I couldn't agree more; we had planned to do it this weekend
if things hadn't unfolded the way they did in Suva.

      We own this house.

And that's the bit you couldn't comprehend: that we weren't tenants.

      But the Fijian guy, isn't he your partner?

As if melanin was magic that could cancel out mortgage documents,
builder's reports, land deeds, council permissions, rates, and all that insurance.

As if families like ours whose Māori and Fijian words float over your fence
are disqualified from something you think is only for people like you.

      No, he's my husband. And we own this house.

I wanted to pick up baby, and I wanted to pick a fight:
the eternal Waitangi *Day dilemma.*

But more than that, I didn't want to be made to feel uncomfortable
about a tree, or home ownership, or being Māori, *or marrying someone from Fiji.*

The slow-motion genocide that is life under siege in a settler colony
is undertaken by quiet conversations, small unbreakable silences, comments left to fester,

an expectation of neighbourliness that means it's okay to assume we don't own a house
but it would be rude for me to draw attention to your assumption.

179 years sat there between us, looking from one side of the fence to the other,
wondering who would make the next move.

(No move is your move, or at least it scores a point for you.)

       Why did you think we were tenants?

You said something illogical but it didn't matter:
we both knew what had gone on here.

Despite everything, I smiled to myself: I had decided to write a Waitangi *poem today.*
I'd been thinking about metaphors while I sped through acres of literal violence:

So many Waikato *killing fields, farms on stolen land drenched with Banaban bones,*
past the faded sign for a café called Cook's Landing.

And then the poem walked out to the car
as soon as it heard me pull in the driveway.

relative

1.   *small*

seeds tucked away, water stored, some dogs, a few rats
look into the faces of relatives you will not see again for several hundred years

sit quietly at night
surrounded by constellations and a dizzying stretch of liquid

ocean-going vessels, blood vessels;
water and genealogy mix in our part of the world

2.   *smaller*

our poi *make the sound of the horses which were met by children*

our poi *make*
the sound of the horses
which were met by children

our	poi	*make*
the	*sound*	*of*
the	*hor*	*ses*
which	*were*	*met*
by	*child*	*ren*

whenever we recall the day the Crown morally defeated itself
we play a trick on time

become our own ancestors and our own descendants:
we are those little kids,
we hold their poi

3.   *smallest*

Shrink-wrapped, vacuum-packed, disassembled, sold for parts,
butt of jokes, scapegoats, too this for that, too that for this,
gravy trains, too angry, special treatment, let it go,
mocked for not possessing the things that have been stolen,
invisible

4.   *scale*

you see a small island
we see the oceanic stretch of Kupe's arrival and promise to return

you see a room at the base of an apartment block
we see what's peeking through a hole in the sheet draped over this whenua

you see us in the city and assume we are far from home
we trace the tracks of our tūpuna as we move with lattes and earphones

our ocean-going navigating vessels
will not fit
the whare you've built to house them

La Mujer

(for Carlos, Carlos and Jorge)

La Malinche
is everywhere tonight:

upstairs in wet Wellington
three of her sons
bear traces of her body;

some part of her lingers
            just outside the rhythm
            just beyond the sound of the language she was first to learn.

La Malinche
is everywhere tonight:

female eyes peer out from my t-shirt
purchased by a friend
at a Zapatista fundraising shop
somewhere in those mountains
where coffee and ideas are thickly brewed;

my friend feared the top wouldn't fit
            but it's the picture
            that's out of place,
            and yet at home,
            on these Ātiawa curves.

La Malinche
is everywhere tonight:

here as well as there
the sounds of stealing and translations
            get louder,
            not softer,
            as they echo down the centuries.

Permeable

(for Cyprus)

A star hangs ominously over this town.
Nearby, a moon waxes and wanes with precision.
On the island of Aphrodite's birth
these signs have nothing to do with beginnings or love.

Things happened here the year your sister was born in a pōhutukawa *season*:
a glacial, tidal, rupturing swell; the rapid displacement of memories.
Families in houses on this sloping flowery street
wondered where the line would stop and if they'd be swallowed up too.

The edges of states, policed by bullet-proof vests
bits of paper
and the stories we remember to tell.

Your Mohawk friend only needs his Status card to roam all over North America.
Unidentifiable bodies strewn each year in Arizona's desert sand.
Guards from the Mexico-US border train Israeli guards against Palestine.
Hysterical appeals from the British National Front:
they're Indigenous; they are overrun by outsiders too.

And on this small island?

Earlier today you looked down an alleyway to another country.
(Unimaginable for a child of the liquid continent.)

Close up: border patrol and EU branding.
In the middle: UN-blue sheeting either side of the path.
At the other end: another booth with a starry flag
and a street that continues the one on which you stood.

Never such an easy border to cross.
Never before a border crossing that made you turn and walk away.

Tonight a band from Greece is in town.
You can hear them over here on Achilleos Avenue –
reverberations of a summer concert under the stars.
The Hellenic syllables of this Cypriot crowd surely echo on that lighted hill too.

A rude traveller, music:
gatecrashing bordercrossing flowing
to the other side.

worst place to be a pilot

watching west papua on tv
but they don't say that:
the british voice-over guy keeps calling it indonesia.

the show is about young english pilots
who fly planes around dramatic mountains:
there are opportunities here they didn't have at home.

new routes are added every year between west papua
and the rest of indonesia:
young white men enabling the spread of things they don't understand.

'we are the people bringing them freedom'
says a 38-year-old with a well-ironed shirt:
'it's like the glory days; it's like catch me if you can.'

i wonder what reality tv show they would have made
in 1840 in the far north:
worst place to be a whaler? trader? missionary? chief?

a polynesian woman is watching west papua on tv
her melanesian husband snoring gently beside her:
his wantoks are on the screen, and hers?

nothing changes in the pacific:
except the fact we forget sometimes
in our own   renamed   islands

that we're a part of it.

room

there are captain cooks amongst us too — bullies,
throwing their weight around

they think they are the centre of the room but that's only because
they have never been anywhere but there
they have no idea about the edges or even how far the room extends
one day they will realise that we in the corners are really in other centres
they will realise there are no corners
no walls

is it a room? is it a room then, when there are no walls?

i used to want to tell them to move over because they take up all the room
but there's no room
there is no room

no walls, no room — just links and connections and space

you're not at the centre; there are no centres
you're just standing there
one node in a massive network
like the rest of us

Mahi

Our love for our disciplines, our hope
for the future but also a real hurt and
struggle in that day to day, working
within a university system.

— *Jacinta* Ruru *on* <u>Ngā Kete Mātauranga</u>

Know what you are getting into in
the institution before you get into it.
Be prepared. Always do your homework.

— *Joanna Kidman & Cherie Chu,* `Māori *scholars*
  and the university'

Our job is to make way for people
who are better than us.

— *Epeli Hau'ofa (via Teresia Teaiwa), 'The thing about it Is . . .'*

Too

It's too hot on my porch today:
Toronto sun which was gently diluted in winter months
is burning a hole in the pocket of the day,
pressing into my black clothes;
it's too bright to read Indigenous theory off white paper here.

It's too colonial in my country today:
four sentences, three Māori, two jail terms, one judge, no justice;
a budget which catches the crumbs as they fall off the table,
piling them on laden plates
rather than letting them fall like gentle rain from heaven
to those who have been made to depend upon them.

It's too distracting in my body today:
obsessed and smiling, I try to keep focus;
such depth of connection, such delicate urgent intimacy
such hope
feels inappropriate in these too-hot too-colonial times.

Pick up coffee cup and printed pages, open the screen door, walk back inside.

My eyes take longer to arrive than the rest of me:
they're still adjusted for the brightness outside;
I bump into things, blind, while I wait for my whole self to arrive,
and realise this is the only worthwhile way to proceed anyway —

All of me, all at once:
anger, frustration, cynicism, hope
and, in the centre as well as the outer reaches, love.

time to write   *(for Larry)*

i need ten minutes to write this poem
you need a couple of hours to work on your story

between incoming calls and outgoing flights
the best i can do is steal time from somewhere else

although you'll read a pristine email version of this poem
there's curry from singh's on the page of this handwritten draft

                              there's no time to write, my friend

i've had this pen and paper forever

i started writing this poem in 1840
wrote a little more when the land was confiscated twenty years later
did some editing the day my great-uncle bled to death:
                    italy, 1944, and dressed for the occasion
made up a stanza when our language fell away from my family not long after
added a new line one august when the government apologised to my iwi

                    grandad always told me i'd never see what i wanted
                    that my grandchildren would see the first real change:
                    i used to think he was taunting me
                    now i see my enthusiasm broke his heart before it broke my own;
                    his warning was a form of protection

                              there's no time to write, my friend

          there's no time to write

maybe i won't ever finish this poem
    maybe it's one stanza of a much longer piece
        maybe your story is a chapter
            in a novel
                on a shelf
                    in a room
                        in a house
                            on an island
                                in an ocean

Firsts

Whatever happens next, remember this:
you have been the first.

You didn't plan to be the first; it just happened.

You signed on for twelve weeks of something
for some reason:
passion, ancestry, interest, timetabling.

People in our ocean have been the first for millennia:
the first to plant this,
the first to fish that,
the first to go there,
the first to see what you can do with that bark
once you take it from that tree.

You need someone to be first so that others can be second,
and third,
and fourth,
and all the way down
until there are so many that it feels
like the firsts had planned to be first:
that they knew what was to come.

But if you asked the firsts
they would say they were giving something a go,
trying something out,
solving a problem,
asking a question:
that it was a big risk, or a small coincidence.

And if you asked the firsts
        they would say they're not the first anyway:
                they would point to the people and reasons and ideas and inheritance
            and — yes, Epeli — the common people and gods:
                all the other firsts that came before.

A decade or a hundred years from now
        what traces will there be of these short weeks spent together?
            Will anyone recall our discussions, our assignments, our names?

Whatever happens next, remember this:
        this is our sea of small decisions, big risks and maybe even coincidences
            that turned out to be history-making
                to be vast
                    to be oceanic.

debris   (for Arini, *with a nod to* Tuwhare)

she's stacking letters side by side: arranging words on a page
coffee tea a bottle of water a plate with crumbs

piles of brightly coloured plastic folders
a shoebox of stationery supplies.

sore red eyes,
an ache for sleep.

a carver, she has found her tupuna *waiting in so many leaves of paper*
a weaver, she has drawn aho *and* whenu *together and smoothed edges into line*

all of that is finished now: completed, done

a scholar, she can't throw the leftovers to the cat: can't burn or rebury them
wants to fashion a new thing from their small and perfect forms

Te Kawa a Māui *farewell*

1. Home

I've never been the ahi kā *kind of girl*
Someone always stays home,
      But someone has to go fish, garden, collect, trade, intermarry, fight

Home is always at the centre
      but we each find the orbit from which we can make our best contribution
            and me? I've never been the ahi kā girl.

2. Okioki

People like us get from Hawaiki to Taranaki via a whirlpool
      and need somewhere
          to get things straightened out again.

When you first arrive you're obsessed
      with wind, water,
          the feeling of being out of control
After some time you focus on what needs to be repaired,
      what can be reused,
          what's too damaged to keep
One day you wake up
      and realise that you can't remember
          which scrape produced which scar
But also that it doesn't matter anymore.

One day you remember that the thing you've been repairing is a waka.

3. Māui

So much depends on the humble macron: a small flat hat
with the ability to change everything.

Somedays Māui *is a guy who fished up islands here, who named an island there*
Somedays Māui *is the name of a house of learning*
Somedays Mauī *is left*

To twist and stretch the language, we might say:
   She's left a house of learning here for a house of learning there.
   There's nothing left.
   This feels like the opposite of right.

  4. **Wāhine** *wing*

A cluster of Māori *women with PhDs*
From all over the tribal and disciplinary map

Cups of tea and doorside conversations: these I will remember.

No, this is not a backhanded comment about Māori *men;*
It's a front-handed comment about Māori *women.*

  5. Hitched

Hitching posts aren't supposed to be forever

Just ask the Wellington City Council (or don't) —
   It's all very well floating a waka for all to see
     But after a while the wood will rot and, if uncarefully dried,
      will split.

The harbour feels safer than the open sea,
   But only as long as you're in denial about the risk of being smashed against the wharf
   Only as long as you force yourself to stop dreaming about life beyond Te Au-a-Tāne
   Only as long as you're happy with shallow breaths and restless nights

Sometimes being hitched is a comfort,
   and sometimes it's a tether, a whip, a noose.

One person's hitch is another person's freedom
        which is another person's incarceration.

6. Still

Some days I long to be still.
But,
I've never been an ahi kā *kind of girl.*

This isn't bragging, and isn't jealousy.
It's not a hang-up, an anxiety or a cry for attention.
This isn't a value judgement, or criticism, or PR.

It's just how it is.
It's just who we are, collectively, together: some are ahi kā, *some roam.*

7. Seven

Although there are seven deadly sins,
And some say seven stars in Matariki,
Someone told me on Wednesday that seven is God's perfect number.

Seven — well, whitu *— is the number of cards I dealt to* Matiu *and myself*
Last nite as we played UNO amid packed boxes in my Waiwhetū *lounge.*

Seven years at Vic, and Matiu *is seven years old.*

My career and nephew are an unusual pair:
        Both standing on own feet for now,
        Both surrounded by layers and layers of people
                More than either he or I will ever know.

from aotearoa to turtle island

(for NSM and Kateri, and for Curnow et al.)

you told us about
old people surrounded by death
two hundred years ago
who designed cradleboards
for not-yet-born generations

what makes death-soaked people quietly embellish care for an unknown baby?

hunched over a typewriter
you smoothed and reinforced supple cords
dreamed they would one day knot
around infant shapes
of unborn unknown genealogies

what made you gently close the door and lovingly coax a ream of paper to life?

another kind of cradle:
a woven beaded basket
and a baby who slept in hers until
she was old enough to wake, roll over,
and walk around with it still tied to her back
cruising around the house,
so her father laughed,
like a small turtle

how do we walk upright?

a large flat stone
is set in the floor of a longhouse
on a campus
for those who need their feet on the ground

wearing the basket you wove
an unknown child of unexpected genealogy
a turtle on a turtle
finds a place to stand

the radical act of sleeping

i. a kapa blanket

of all the unfolding and gentle handling
in this archive room
the most surprising sheets
were tapa – kapa – an expanse of beaten fibre
sewn to a stretch of red cotton
patterns pounded into kapa still visible on the cotton as well
layers of kapa for insulation in between:
under which a Hawaiian family slept almost 200 years ago
a paperbark Eskimo pie

ii. a flag blanket

families gifted quilts to children:
rows of Hawaiian flags arching across the roof
one end of a long dorm room to the other
a double pattern of love and allegiance
to a school-bound boy
and a kingdom

iii. perhaps this is the radical act

the sovereignty
the activism:
to keep our children safe
as they sleep

Fryer Library, UQ

You sit in an air-conditioned archive
Working your way through boxes of paper
Underneath a picture of David Unaipon
And you don't feel as lonely
In this university place
As you have felt in others
Surrounded by people

An Indigenous scholar's request to other scholars

1.   *Engage[1] with[2] my[3] scholarship.[4]*
2.   *Engage[5] with[6] scholarship[7] by other[8] Indigenous[9] scholars.[10]*
3.   *Yep that's pretty much it.[11]*

---

[1] *Treat it as scholarship with which you as a scholar can engage: do not treat it as (or refer to it as) perspective or culture; do not assume that the articulation of an intellectual difference from my arguments would cause, produce or have anything to do with offence. Your bibliography shows who you have been reading — so do your comments and your arguments.*

[2] *Read what has been written, assume that what you're writing on might have been written on by Indigenous people, and consider that there is no reason to think about Indigenous participation in scholarly conversation as necessarily being any different than participation by any other people in scholarly conversations. (Except that not being engaged with is a special and unique privilege accorded to Indigenous scholars all the time, and bears striking resemblance to the centuries-old practice of assuming Indigenous people are not present.)*

[3] *The scholarship produced by me with all of its disciplinary, personal, institutional, contextual and formal specificity — please do not refer to 'Indigenous scholars' as if all of our work is the same or about the same things. My name is Alice Te Punga Somerville (please do not assume that Te Punga is a middle*

name — if you are not sure how to cite or refer to me or alphabetise an index or list of conference presenters or book an airline ticket for me, I am happy to clarify that my last name starts with a 'T') and my work, like the work of all scholars, is connected to my own unique set of circumstances, experiences, training and inheritance.

[4] *By scholarship I mean publications, presentations and other public writing and discussion. By publications I mean books, journal articles, book chapters, creative work.*

[5] *See note 1.*
[6] *See note 2.*

[7] *See note 4. Additionally, for a whole lot of reasons you and I both know, there are reasons that Indigenous scholars have had (and continue to have) less access to certain kinds of publication venues. Even after considering the large number of books, articles and chapters written by Indigenous scholars you may find a great deal of Indigenous scholarship in research theses, reports, book reviews, oral presentations, interviews and other less conventional (and yet still scholarly) spaces. Consider that there might be scholarship relevant to your discipline or research area that has been*

published or presented in interdisciplinary (including Indigenous Studies) or other disciplinary spaces: make good use of your library's search engine or google scholar if you feel flummoxed about the question of how to find scholarship by Indigenous scholars. Imagine that an Indigenous scholar from your discipline may be in a 'Studies' department elsewhere on your very own campus.

[8] I am not ever the only Indigenous scholar; actually, no Indigenous scholar is ever the only Indigenous scholar. Indigenous scholars are part of vast networks globally: there is, consequently, a sense of community as well as a sense of multiplicity in the Indigenous scholarly world. Scholarship that does not engage this wide range of scholarship misses out on the opportunity to make the most of the intellectual work — which may or may not be about Indigenous topics — in which Indigenous scholars are engaged.

[9] By Indigenous, I mean people who are Indigenous to the specific land where we/you are located as well as Indigenous to the nation state where we/you are located as well as Indigenous to another space on the globe on which we/you are located. There are so many Indigenous scholars in such a wide range of disciplines, institutions, countries and career stages

that it is exhausting (as well as exhilarating) trying to keep up with all of the scholarship being produced by them/us. Looking for Indigenous scholarship does not make you a member of the identity police: you will find that when an Indigenous scholar wants you to know they are Indigenous they will let you know — in their writing, in their contributor/biographical notes, in their university websites, in their acknowledgements and introductions.

[10] Many Indigenous scholars have doctoral and/or masters-level research training; for reasons that you and I both understand there are fewer Indigenous scholars with these degrees than any of us would like. You have an opportunity to use whatever power you have to engage with the work of, draw attention to, and even train, Indigenous scholars. This is a win-win: you get to benefit from the wonderful intellectual contribution of even more Indigenous scholars, and Indigenous scholars get to be treated like scholars. Next step: an opportunity to argue for permanent academic hires of Indigenous scholars across your own institutions.

[11] If you are seeking absolution, guilt-reduction, or to think harder about your place in the academy, please refer to points one and two. We have written about all of that too.

Swipe left

Took Imperialism home for a shag
And what a long night of tangled sheets that turned out to be:
Nothing approaching the making of love
But a whole lot of gratuitous kink
That left us both exhausted in the morning.

Had an on-again off-again thing with gender:
Gender gets me horny
Gets me to a place where I'm ashamed to be so desperate:
During the wild ride of fully consenting ravenous limbs
I always forget that afterwards we have to lie there and talk
So I sneak out while gender's sleeping
Avoid gender's eye when we bump into each other at the supermarket.

My friend with benefits used to be culture
But culture was pretty needy
So now I've got class on my speed dial:
Class is great — you can tell people whatever you want
About how and why you and class get it on
Don't need to provide corroborating evidence or paternity tests
Just a nice slow screw in the back of a beaten-up car.

Had a one-night stand with race
And it was true, what I'd heard from mates who'd taken race for a spin:
Race likes to do it in public
And though I tried to get extra kicks from the fear of being found out
I was most scared of myself finding me there.

One day I want to settle down

But for now I'm having way too much fun
Playing the field.

kia tūpato

don't apologise for not speaking our language as well as me
don't imply my feeble response to our humiliations
is a sign of unfair proximity

don't make me into a cardboard cutout

don't step onto that museum plinth
with a carefully typed label already in place
about being flung between two worlds

don't hang yourself out to dry

don't stand outside everyone's houses
nose pressed against cold glass
breath making clouds —
> *not when the windows of this* whare *(this fale this vale) may be closed*
> *but the door right next to them is wide open*

don't turn us into the bad guys

this white audience
slurps up your brown tears
which you artistically, publicly, painfully, freely shed
> *for the obscuring*
> *of their sins*

tau(gh)t

the fine line between kaupapa and kūpapa
is the taut string of a pūrerehua in flight

which is to say,

the vibration of something bigger than all of us
that can thrum to the pulse of the universe
or slice to the bone

Missing

I miss those of you who have twisted words into ropes for our people.
Had you spliced your cords to the woven lengths the rest of us were making,
Instead of showing off your own lovely strands,
We could have slowed the sun.

a symposium, sixteenth-century style
(for Te Pouhere Kōrero)

they   don't know how to draw
           the lines on the map:
           tracing paper and pencils
           unable to mark
           contours shaped by pouwhenua
           rather than borders

they   don't know about the boxes
           stored under stairs:
           long recordings, bits of paper
           chicken scratches and angles
           hours of propped-up eyelids
           while last breaths and sound
           connect just in time
           to save the ones
           yet to come

they   don't see the bayonets
           their words and methods become
           in our hands:
           slicing flesh
           sometimes to kill,
           sometimes to send a loved one home

but that's enough about them

we   are what we map
           we are what we box
           we're the map, the box,
           the new black.

Titaua's ship

(for Titaua Porcher)

another time we saw you:
you arrived on your ship
loaded with tapa and other gifts
from your home

you spent time talking genealogy:
catching up and trading stories
with relatives you hadn't seen
for generations

you came with tapa in sheets of impossible size:
proof of what we'd thought were grandparents' myths
about our shreds of paperbark
stories of Hawaiki.

we knew you'd brought the ship to come and find us:
next time Cook came
we asked him where you were —

we've waited for your return.

this time,
your ship was shaped like a lecture theatre —
once again it was loaded with things from your home

though they all spoke with confidence about the cargo in their hold,
and I couldn't understand a word you said,
I know this is
Titaua's ship

one day, e hoa,
this won't be a ship anymore:
one day
this will be our waka

Aroha

. . . I heard
your spirit wailing as it flew
　　　over my head, seeking faraway Reinga.
— *Alistair* Te Ariki *Campbell, 'Death of a Friend'*

Apirana *wanted us to have a last look at*
each other. He was standing on the steps
of the plane with a smile on his face as he
waved. I waved and smiled back, and we
both stood perfectly still for a moment as
we gazed across the intervening space at
each other. It was a long look which carried
a message of the love and affection which
had existed between us for over fifty years
of unclouded friendship. Then Apirana
turned to enter his plane and I went inside
to await mine. We had had our last look.

— Te Rangihiroa *(Sir Peter Buck),* 'He Poroporoaki
　　— *A Farewell Message'*

first draft of a waiata tangi

(for Te Rangihiroa)

it's hot here:
without electric fan, open window, bare legs
i'd be lying in the dark, heavy-limbed and drowsy

as it is, i can feel an ache of warmth at the back of my neck
where hair falls in a tight curtain around an already moist little nook
i'm lying on my tummy, skin pressing into a warm patch of blanket
working on the first draft of something i'll never finish

although warmed milk and sheets are supplied at night-time
to wide-awake children in the islands of our births
warmth has the opposite effect here:
it's too hot to fall quickly to sleep tonight.

i visited your whare te pātaka o pihopa *today*

before heading to the archive in the back of the building
i walked through front doors, up stairs, over carpet
to greet the small māori *display at the end of the mezzanine*

laid a handful of leaves beside the whakairo *there*
quietly sang to them under my breath,
a small one-sided karanga
surprising the other occupants more than the other visitors

wondered if you used to visit these cabinets too
if you looked across the carpet as i did and felt them looking back,
appraising,
gluing feet to floor and tumbling body into air,
all at the same time

walked along corridors you paced for years,
a precise producer of catalogues:
a scientist working with the test tubes and bunsen burners of culture
before it was embarrassing to treat people like lab rats,
to steal things and ideas for safekeeping on air-conditioned shelves

the relief it must have been to return here after your last trip home,
but also the grief:

did you visit the whakairo *more or less after your final wrenching?*
does spending time with those things of our own provide solace or discomfort?
do things behind glass feel enclosed, cut off, pristine, or do they keep you company?

e te rangihiroa

still hot, still sticky:
was it like this the night you died?

i wonder if you felt more at home as your body turned cold after last breaths

i wonder if your wairua *found a path to follow to* hawaiki,
departing as it did from this wrong end of our marvellous watery hemisphere

traffic

(for Epeli Hau'ofa, January 2009)

radio news: there are floods in fiji
liquid pouring into dry places

rain and currents giving nadi an unexpected bath:
next she'll be dressed in clothes of movement and mud

telecom washes its hands of the phone calls that aren't getting through:
the cords between here and there have been cut and we must wait for reconnection

a new year spent driving to beaches with young nephews and their talk of king tides:
each night they announce tomorrow will be the big one

but we adults know a real king tide is seasonal, occasional, extraordinary, rare:
the reminder that water chooses its own edges in our part of the world

something's leaking in my inbox:
email traffic about the passing of a tōtara

in some parts of the world they might say your spirit is now adrift:
but in floods, during tides of extraordinary depth, huge tōtara logs tend to float instead

you're still criss-crossing, epeli
still traversing our deep and watery home

te ariki

(for Alistair Te Ariki Campbell)

go now, e te ariki,
to your mates, your beloved, your blood

let those hands which held all those pens
magicked a thousand thousand words
lie still and empty at last

go back home
with no return ticket this time
spend no more nights dreaming of an infancy in the sun
your mother has been waiting for you

go the way your friends have gone;
the tracks may still be warm from hone's *recent journey:*
you've been one of us on these rugged frozen isles
since arriving with a luggage tag on your small boy's jacket
all those years ago;
you and your brother fighting alongside us
since before we can remember,
one in the 28th, the other on pages;
the least we can do is loan you a pathway home

no longer perch on the edge of these cliffs with an eye on the tide:
follow sand to water,
leave us behind,
go

alistair te ariki *campbell:*
firsts and firsts
accomplishments
and now you've breathed your last

Sphere

(for J. C. Sturm and my lockdown baby)

> 'The planet is an urupā' — J. C. Sturm

I am a planet.
My tides, my orbit, my atmosphere,
my seasons, my poles, my girth.

When I saw a pulse on the screen —
a heartbeat deep in my womb —
you became my Rūaumoko:
Shaking everything —
nausea, vertigo, vomit, sleep.

Three days after we buried you at home
in a box with a butterfly on its lid
I felt the deep rumble and sharp jolt
of that unborn child
still tucked inside its mother.

Yes, I am jealous of Papatūānuku who,
despite everything, at least still has her child.

I am a planet:
Swirling oceans;
Sharp rock;
A molten core.

I am a planet:
longing to be in the sweet spot
between too cold and too hot
for life.

I am an urupā:
full of whakapapa, *full of death,*
quiet;
a place to mourn the hearts
that used to beat
here.

he waiata tangi, he waiata aroha

(after the wreck of the Rena — for Tangaroa)

this drifting isn't swimming, isn't flight:
these scales and feathers, gills, beaks and eyes
meant for water, salt and wind; not
the quiet surge and flow of thicker tides

when pressed under rock and time, oil
transubstantiates into diamonds, but
this is the wrong pressure, these are not enough years
an oozing has obscured your cut and sheen

sometimes stillness is a sign of strength
the quiet calm of infinite depth, but
there is no reflection on this liquid skin
breaths, mouths, even words are too shallow here

An Indigenous woman scholar's prayer

(for Teresia Teaiwa and Tracey Banivanua Mar)

May I grow old enough to be forgotten.

May my questions become passé,
    may my bibliographies become outdated,
        may my theories be superseded,
            may I be obsolete.

May I teach students who teach students who teach students:
    may I meet these younger thinkers at conferences,
        may I read and cite their work,
            may I watch them stand more stably than I could ever have
            dreamed.

May I sit in committee meetings where young colleagues raise new challenges
    because the old ones have finally been put to rest.

May I watch the old guard quietly move on, but more than this:
    may I live long enough to be part of an old guard
        who younger scholars wish would retire.
            (May I get to retire.)

May I see scores of Indigenous scholars
    write hundreds of Indigenous books
        that ask thousands of Indigenous questions.

May I meet Indigenous vice-chancellors, presidents, professors, and deans;
    may they not all be men.

May I lie on a future deathbed and look back with regrets related to work
    rather than regrets related to family.

May my passing be unshocking, not early, not unexpected.

May I run out of ideas before I run out of time.

Ngā Mihi

I was raised by a whānau of readers and taught by scholars who were also poets. I have read, and heard, and learned alongside thinkers with questions that changed the way I see the world.

So much of my writing has been related to my academic life — thank you to those who have encouraged me to also write and share poetry. At key moments there have also been writing communities — especially teachers and fellow students of the University of Auckland Creative Writing paper 1998, Brandy Nālani McDougall and our kai-and-poetry sessions while I was in Honolulu 2003–4, and the Writer's Block whānau in Wellington which I joined in 2006.

My decision to be — and to continue to be — an academic involves plenty of privileges and good days, but also racism, isolation and a complete lack of work-life balance. I will never forget my sister Megan packing tiny Matiu into the baby capsule to pick me up, crying, from campus just weeks into my first academic job — she took me to Cobb & Co. Petone and helped me regain perspective after I had just run headlong into the first of many, many walls. Too many relatives, friends and colleagues have spent too many hours listening, sharing, reflecting, encouraging and raging with me — face to face and online — as I have unpacked and repacked the cost of writing while colonised.

Special thanks to those editors and publications that have brought some of these poems into the world before now: Hinemoana Baker, 4th Floor Literary Journal, 2013; Anton Blank, Ora Nui 1, 2012 and Ora Nui 2, 2014; Winnie Dunn, Cordite Poetry Review 100, 2021; Fiona Farrell, Ōrongohau | Best New Zealand Poems, 2018; Paula Green, NZ Poetry Shelf, 2021; Tahu Kukutai, Law Text Culture 15 (1), 2011; Tina Makereti, Magical Māori Mystery Tour of Wellington, 2017; Mark Pirie, Broadsheet: New New Zealand Poetry 9, 2011–12; Maraea Rakuraku & Vana Manasiadis, Tatai Whetū: Seven Māori Women Poets in Translation, Seraph Press, 2018; Albert Wendt, Reina Whaitiri & Robert Sullivan, Mauri Ola: Contemporary Polynesian Poems in English, AUP, 2010; Reina Whaitiri & Robert Sullivan, Puna Wai Kōrero: An Anthology of Māori Poetry in English, AUP, 2014; Lesley Wheeler, Shenandoah 62 (2), 2013. Ngā mihi nui to Jolisa Gracewood and Hineitimoana Greensill who have cast expert eyes over final drafts.

Finally, thank you to clear-eyed, deep-hearted Vula. This collection is dedicated to our creative stubborn hilarious bossy affectionate amazing daughter — inheritor of so much and so many.

Alice Te Punga Somerville (Te Āti Awa, Taranaki) is a
scholar, poet and irredentist. She researches and teaches
Māori, Pacific and Indigenous texts in order to centre
Indigenous expansiveness and de-centre colonialism.
Alice is a professor in the Department of English Language
and Literatures and the Institute for Critical Indigenous
Studies at the University of British Columbia. She studied
at the University of Auckland, earned a PhD at Cornell
University, is a Fulbright scholar and Marsden recipient
and has held academic appointments in New Zealand,
Canada, Hawai'i and Australia. Her first book *Once Were
Pacific: Māori Connections to Oceania* (University of
Minnesota Press, 2012) won Best First Book from the
Native American & Indigenous Studies Association.
Her most recent book is *Two Hundred and Fifty Ways
to Start an Essay about Captain Cook* (BWB, 2020).